BOA
EDITIONS LTD

CLUES FROM THE ANIMAL KINGDOM

D1056707

CLUES FROM THE ANIMAL KINGDOM

POEMS BY CHRISTOPHER KENNEDY

AMERICAN POETS CONTINUUM SERIES, NO. 167
BOA EDITIONS, LTD. ☙ ROCHESTER, NY ☙ 2018

First Edition
18 19 20 21 7 6 5 4 3 2 1

For information about permission to reuse any material from this book, please contact The Permissions Company at www.permissionscompany.com or e-mail permdude@gmail.com.

Publications by BOA Editions, Ltd.—a not-for-profit corporation under section 501 (c) (3) of the United States Internal Revenue Code—are made possible with funds from a variety of sources, including public funds from the Literature Program of the National Endowment for the Arts; the New York State Council on the Arts, a state agency; and the County of Monroe, NY. Private funding sources include the Lannan Foundation; the Max and Marian Farash Charitable Foundation; the Mary S. Mulligan Charitable Trust; the Rochester Area Community Foundation; the Ames-Amzalak Memorial Trust in memory of Henry Ames, Semon Amzalak, and Dan Amzalak; and contributions from many individuals nationwide. See Colophon on page 112 for special individual acknowledgments.

Cover Design: Daphne Morrissey
Cover Art: Tessa Kennedy
Interior Design and Composition: Richard Foerster
Manufacturing: McNaughton & Gunn
BOA Logo: Mirko

Library of Congress Cataloging-in-Publication Data

Names: Kennedy, Christopher, 1955– author.
Title: Clues from the animal kingdom : poems / by Christopher Kennedy.
Description: First edition. | Rochester, NY : BOA Editions, Ltd., 2018. |
  Series: American poets continuum series ; no. 167
Identifiers: LCCN 2018015161 (print) | LCCN 2018018259 (ebook) | ISBN
  9781942683650 (ebook) | ISBN 9781942683643 (pbk. : alk. paper)
Classification: LCC PS3611.E557 (ebook) | LCC PS3611.E557 A6 2018 (print) |
  DDC 811/.6—dc23
LC record available at https://lccn.loc.gov/2018015161

BOA Editions, Ltd.
250 North Goodman Street, Suite 306
Rochester, NY 14607
www.boaeditions.org
A. Poulin, Jr., Founder (1938–1996)

Contents

I

Confusing Myself with the Whippoorwill   13
Waves and Particles   14
Coaxing the Dog Inside   15
An Old-Fashioned Comedy   16
Between Heaven and Hell   17
A Better Theater Than My Skull   18
Five Fictions   19
Scuola Metafisica   21
Recidivist Rex   22
Postulate   23
Mantras   24
Folk Tale   25
Like Sailboats on TV   26
Midnight Sundial   27
How I Learned to Play Guitar   28
Family Tree   29
Temporal Location Finder   30
The Black Boot, the River, the Burning House   31
Radiant Fish   32

II

The Double Sedative   35
Small Hope Factory   36
The Seeded Light   37
Basement Tapes   38
The Captain of No Team That I Know of   39
A Green Ocean Somewhere Far Away   40

I Have Approximated Lightning 41

Like IHOP at 3:00 A.M., I Radiate 42

City of Shells 43

Factotum 44

Orient 45

Speculation About the Future 46

Big Money for Broken Gold 47

Like Any Other Planet 48

Like Galileo 49

The Grand Kinetic Neon Macabre 50

Some Other Species of Love 51

My Strategy 52

Reading Celan on Labor Day 53

Cow Hill, Bull Hill 54

III

Death Metal Sunset 57

Mourning, Not Rending 58

Above the Ashes 59

Like a Dog Barking at a Statue of the Virgin Mary 60

The Natural World 61

Like a Werewolf on the Moon 62

The Ghost 63

Aegis in Abstentia 64

The Beautiful Zoo Where No One Says I Love You 65

These Thoughts of Existence 66

Halloween 67

The Chaos Each Night Brings 68

Chrysalis 69

Sustainability 70

Searching for Terry Melcher 71

There Is a Word I Keep Forgetting 72

Algorithm   75
North Island   76
Graveyard, Root, and Forest   77

IV

Clues from the Animal Kingdom   81
Monstrous   83
Zen Portraiture   84
At Brooklyn Pickle   85
Marital   86
Sinkhole in Knife Town   87
Orange Sunshine   88
Quarantine   89
In the Realm of Minor Keys   90
Triptych: Analogy of Faith   91
Against Surrealism   93
Causality   94
My Face Is a Stranger to the Mirror of God   95
Autobiography of an Excised Heart   96
Historical   97
At Least Our Ruins Will Be Spectacular   98
Time Travel   99
Drift and Sway   100
The Hidden Wishes of the Night   101
Visit to a Random Orchard   102
This Pharaoh of I   103

Acknowledgments   *104*
About the Author   *106*
Colophon   *112*

"I thought it was the Inferno but it was Purgatory."

Tomas Tranströmer
translated by Robin Fulton

I

Confusing Myself with the Whippoorwill

Today, I was a madness of regrettable actions. At the convenience store, I eyed the cashiers warily as they slouched in round-shouldered, teenaged aplomb. Their youth not yet wasted.

Try not to think was my mantra as I left through the slow, antagonistic electric doors, but the whippoorwills disturbed me with their calls, despite a 93% decline in their numbers in the Empire State.

And where have they gone? Camouflaged beyond reason so as to be nearly extinct? These questions led me to my own desire to disappear.

At home, filled with envy, I chopped some vegetables to store for later when the seasons have changed and my plumage has darkened, my face of feathers and slanted light, a veritable mirage.

Waves and Particles

I wake from a dream of digging my own grave to the sound of my neighbor who has lost both his legs, shoveling his walk, scraping his metal blade across the bricks that lead to his front door. The violet light of early dawn filters through the bathroom window and reflects off the mirror, a wash of waves and particles. A crow glides toward a dead deer's body on the shoulder of the main highway. Two thousand miles away, a scorpion waits in the sand for a horse to pass, its stinger taut and arched behind its back. I see the black shoe you left behind, fallen to its side. There is no need for life on other planets.

Coaxing the Dog Inside

A black dog looked in my apartment window. Its eyes were as black as its face. Its face as black as a bible. I stared into its bible-black eyes and saw my reflection. I coaxed the dog toward the window. I opened the door and called the dog, whose name I didn't know. The dog came to the door. It entered the apartment, fearful, but driven by hunger. I stared at it, hoping to see myself again. I looked at the dog looking at me, and I understood its curiosity was my own.

I knew the dog was something I'd manifested, something I gave birth to from my skull like a god. Because the dog reminded me of my childhood, I trusted it. The dog shied. I spoke in high, reassuring tones. *Here, boy,* I said. *Here, boy.* It cowered and bared its yellow teeth, its liver-spotted gums. I did not understand the white worms coiled in the blood-slick nest of its heart. I reached to pet it. I was surprised how vicious it was.

An Old-Fashioned Comedy

The television strobe divided the room into halves of poverty and grief. We'd put down the dog but not its fleas. They jumped from the olive-green carpet onto our ankles. The old-fashioned comedy shined on us. The fat man was dressed like a robot; the thin man in a vest gestured relentlessly. There was a red telephone next to the couch like the one that calls Russia at the end of the world. When it rang, we refused to answer. The news was never good. How long could this go on? A long time, but quickly. The clock in the kitchen was fast.

Between Heaven and Hell

From here I see the dim lights of the reactor towers and the moon at the end of its tether. A mother and father wave their children in from the water to the beach, where melancholic flies inspect a half-eaten fish, their Dante-circle shrinking as they lower toward the sun-bleached flesh.

The children dive under, ignoring their parents' calls, as if they've forgotten the names they were given. The parents bolt up from their beach chairs in a mild panic every time the children disappear. I'm forced to watch through the eyes of the animal that brought me here, the animal I'm trapped inside of, confused and untamable, not quite above it all, here, where the timid waves tremble and refuse the shore.

A Better Theater Than My Skull

The cloud, dispersing above me, is a dead bird flying back into an egg. Then it's gone. The moon is a doll's head melting in a bonfire. There is a moment just before sleep when my body lets go, and I'm as empty as a dead man's shoes and old enough to be my own father. The night sky's black flank tattooed with light, the moon comes and goes, its face an indistinguishable horror. I wait for the curtain to rise in a better theater than my skull. A heart is four chambers filled with blood. The dead man sails his coffin across the tops of burning trees.

Five Fictions

Analogous

A boat full of rescuers comes upon a shipwreck whose cargo was several crates of ventriloquist dummies. A number of small heads bob up and down in the waves. The crew thinks they are about to save some children from drowning; instead, as they approach, they see the animated faces of the wooden-headed dolls, their mouths unhinged, opening and closing as the sea water pushes through, as if they can't stop laughing.

Hypothetical

The sky is full of parachutes that float like dandelion seeds. It's impossible to clearly determine the shapes of the bodies that hang from them. Also, impossible to know if this is a time of war or a time of peace.

As the bodies come into better view, it seems that some of them are wearing military uniforms and others are dressed in colorful circus costumes.

It's a pleasant evening. The sky is turning violet and pink. The fields are bright yellow except where the shadows are descending. The flapping of silk stirs a gentle breeze.

A House Seems Quiet

Sometimes breathing is the sound of trees flayed and deboned. I don't know how else to tell you how it feels to be alive. I've seen the young girl's arabesque under tulle and heard death's polite applause. Listen. The leaves whirr like blades across the sky. We herd like frightened beasts against the electric dark. We're all gutted. It feels like we're eating fire. Are we eating fire? The fire knows.

Dead for Skin

It is turning yellow where we live. Not in a seasonal way. More in the way paper curls and ages, turns a burnt shade of white. Leaves and grass tinged with it, not dying, not sun-drenched. No infusion of light.

Where we live, it is sick with a color we can't explain. When we eat, the meal is yellow, jaundiced, and full of bad luck. An arm or leg, covered with light fur, like a succulent piece of fruit, flush with skin that has ripened.

Though we are dead for skin, we eat. It is a hopeful act. We eat. We do not name what we are eating. It is better to keep the animal a secret.

We eat. The taste is familiar. The smell conjuring something even more terrible: a meal from childhood. We eat. But never know what.

Filial Horrors

A noise like animals licking their lips in the night, so that everywhere sounds like the waves of a devouring sea. You hear a noise in an octave like a voice made of glass on Saturn. Your heart is a cosmonaut's charred remains. When you open a window to see what's making all the commotion, you see a bird with a small head that looks just like yours. You utter a warbling sound you've never made before. The bird lifts its wings and flies toward you, shouting, *Father*.

Scuola Metafisica

The dead live in the grooves of old 45s, waiting to become music, and the rush of traffic on the highway is the dead saying good-bye. The slow parade of eyes, watching you walk by, the dead live there, too. In the reckless spin of a knife-tip ballerina, the blood of the world's oldest woman. In the light and shadow that give birth to dislocation, in the statues of antiquity, the green abandoned house where you slept like a rusted engine in an old car, where the fire rose to the roof with the same slow, mechanical movement of a robot's head. The dead there in all of it. When you speak to the dead, you speak to yourself. You say, *I was Asleep. Now I am Awake. Look how I have grown.*

Recidivist Rex

Bleach cleanses nothing permanently. Plumes of smoke hang in the air like question marks. Mine is a cleansing anger. You lose value every day, by choice, by a simple exertion, by rolling up your sleeves. Before your next act of oblivion, consider the consequences; then proceed to smash another guitar. When you're in your go-go coma, I won't be visiting. I prefer to see you standing, lightning-fingered, the days scattered behind you like burnt matches in the snow.

Postulate

Today the traffic is sparse, the sky nearly white in its pale blue mask. The wind in the trees gives me a sound to listen to like an animal running through the tall grass when I'm alone.

Inside the sky, oceans scar the sun. I plan to remake you, to rescue you from the no-one-knows, the prayer of what will be when we are gone. I look for you under collapsed umbrellas in the rain. I look for you to prove the theory of dust to dust. To prove what needs no proof.

How did I feel when I heard you were gone?

Picture a hunter's moon above a white barn, the barn on fire, the yellow flames, straining toward the moon. Then the sound no one could ever forget, the sound of burning horses, moonlight branded on their blistering flanks.

Mantras

These are the trees risen from nowhere, the flood breaching the riverbed, the sledge, the cow's inadequate skull. This is where I set the hills on fire, the smoke whisking my lungs. This is the shadow of a blue heron, prehistoric and grim, and there is the heron, searing its gaze into my eyes. I dreamed these hours that have come true when old houses extinguish, and the women who own them fall asleep inside the beads of their rosaries. I wanted a mantra of one syllable that would release me, as if stricken by a surge of lightning in the purple sky. I wanted an Aztec shimmer on this leaden world. But there was only thunder and the animals that listened for prey in the night. The dead saying, *not yet*. My tired arms gathering headstones together to build my sturdy home.

FOLK TALE

I ran down the highway's yellow lines in my sleep last night. When I woke up, your skin was a desert with no oasis. When I was a boy, the crack of the barber strap used to wake me up, but someone stole it and threw it on the roof of the Brown & Jewel.

My mother said my father lost his paycheck in a poker game and came home and cried at her feet. I colored eggs that Easter like a fool. I fed a horse some grass and another boy lost his finger. My father borrowed a brand-new car and never came back. The Lord works in mysterious ways, but it all adds up.

Once, I dreamed the ace of spades was a dagger.

Like Sailboats on TV

Across from the charred white bar and grill, in the place where the Irish still bury their dead, I stood next to your grave. Looking at it then, it didn't seem so final.

There was a light that fell across the marker the amber color of an empty pill bottle.

And the distance was false.

You were gone but here, like the picture you took of sailboats on TV. Like the handwriting on a letter you wrote in 1961.

As the light faded, my vision narrowed, and I saw the grave had grown four legs and a long, prehensile tail.

I watched as it crawled away, a green, stone-headed creature, in a halo of blue whatever.

MIDNIGHT SUNDIAL

My eleven windows are sheets of ice. A clutter of white spiders runs across the blue shadow of the moon. My shadow is lost in their shadows. Time can't see itself in the mirror. I sleep inside my own head, a shame substitute for sunrise when I wake and wonder where I am. It will be raining, and I will be late for everything. The hills are plumb tonight in the curse-kiss of absence, in rain spore and lamp shadow. A million furnaces in melancholy galaxies burn out where suicides outnumber births, land of the dead where expediency trumps romance. To reach it, I have to swim the depths of all the bottomless seas in my sleep. The only way to reach extinguished stars.

How I Learned to Play Guitar

I buried the guitar in a shallow grave in the backyard. I returned to the house and lit several candles arranged haphazardly on the kitchen table. I sat and watched the wax melt and pool. Red pools. White pools.

When the candles burned down, I walked outside and dug up the guitar. I removed the strings and hung them from the branch of a large maple tree. I carried the guitar inside and smashed it to pieces on the floor. I gathered the splintered wood and put it in the oven. I turned on the oven and watched the wood through the small window in the oven door.

After several minutes, the wood began to smolder. I opened the oven door and removed the wood. I carried the pieces outside and set them on the grass. I fanned them until they caught on fire. I watched them burn. I ran my fingers up and down the strings that were swaying back and forth on the branch in a light breeze. It began to rain. I stood there for a while. I mimicked the act of playing guitar.

The next day, I bought a new instrument. I put the fingers of my right hand on strategic places along the neck. I strummed with my left. I began to weep.

The song I played is called what's wrong with me.

Family Tree

I watched the Christmas tree fly sideways like an arrow onto the lawn. Lights and bulbs cracking, a missile aimed at sorrow. There was a halo around the moon. A streetlight flickered above the boulevard. My mother stood on the stoop, breathing hard, so that I could see she was alive. Not everyone was. And anyways the slipknot comfort of the past is just another noose, hanging from an old catalpa.

I never saw my shadow then when it wasn't being eaten by the shade, and looking back, it's gone, replaced by a mutant shape. The sky sparks briefly in the distance tonight, stagnant with heat. I kill the time that's killing me, nirvana-starved, calm, meditating on the mute indifference of the room, becoming so small I could be eaten by a flea—but I grow like a seed into the tree of myself, rooted, a rope around my sturdy neck.

TEMPORAL LOCATION FINDER

I walked through a seemingly endless field with a woman covered with bees. A child covered with scorpions followed. The woman raised her arm, and some of the bees rose up slightly and hovered before settling back on her bare skin. After we walked a few miles, we found ourselves in what appeared to be the middle of the field. We met a man covered with vultures, and I asked him where to go next. The man, who was lying on his back, pointed east and west, and when I asked him which way we should go, the man said nothing. *I've heard of this,* I said, *but I never thought I'd live to see it.* I looked behind me and there stood the bee woman and the scorpion child. They seemed to be waiting to see what would happen next. A few more vultures flew toward the supine man and landed on his head. *So this is death,* I said, and the woman and the child shook their heads carefully so as not to disturb the things that defined them. I looked right then left, in the opposite directions the man's arms suggested, and it was obvious to me then where the field began and ended.

THE BLACK BOOT, THE RIVER, THE BURNING HOUSE

Here the silence of trees is louder than God and the mute girl has wandered away. Here, the black boot, the river, the burning house. The willows bent over in the storm like weary travelers. The pack of dogs asleep on the doorstep. The noise in the basement. The hollowed-out gourd we used as a pipe. The police car in the driveway at night like a spaceship. The mute girl returned to her father, who paced in the kitchen while we watched through the window. The moon, beautiful as ivory, and hidden behind the clouds. The story we were told and the truth we knew. The mute girl's hands as she signed. The way her fingers screamed.

Radiant Fish

The sun rose and set in the context of the wounded lake, like a radiant fish, breaking the surface of spume and algae. A fisherman waved his free hand as if to welcome me. I waved back the way strangers try to reassure other strangers. I said your name like a mantra, like the music of a body pressed against another body until the music drifted and faded. I heard in the silence the glittery click of vanished stars. I waved back to reassure, but it was clear I was saying good-bye.

The Double Sedative

Complicated sky this evening—chemical loneliness of fallen rain, wet dirt of the flowerbed, as if a corpse were about to dig itself out of the earth. Warm from the night's unseasonable temperature, I open the door to the frogs' harrumphs, pulsing like alien heartbeats.

On TV, in the cop show, palm trees line the entrance to the gentlemen's club, its silver welcome like a postcard from suicide, written in the spangly cursive of a teenage diarist.

And it's not as if I can ever decipher things, learn their origins, their meanings, sugar myself a certainty, as the mountains in the distance represent permanence though they slowly erode.

I can only stand here dumbly, my heart cold and heavy like a boat full of snow, my love scenes like murder scenes, my murder scenes like love scenes, and listen as the howls rise in the throats of whatever beasts are drawing near.

SMALL HOPE FACTORY

We were always the hopeful ones, thrilled to find a cigarette still burning in the grass. It felt good to have a pocket full of change and nowhere to go. I found a coupon for get one free of something. It didn't matter what. Payday was magical and came once a week, like church. The world was a poignant and miraculous place. A job, any job, was good and life-affirming.

My family was a factory of small hopes. I dreamed I found a pile of quarters in the neighbor's grass and brought them to my grateful mother. When I woke up, I had the feeling I could be anything I wanted to be. First light was shining through the venetian blinds. I heard Elvis singing "Hound Dog." I started singing along. I couldn't wait until we all sat down for breakfast, so I could spoon some sugar from the white bowl on my cereal. There was talk of a new car. Someday, maybe. I thought if I started to run, I could run around the world.

I saw my father in the yard. I grabbed my glove and took off the rubber band. The pocket was deep and dark where I rubbed in the neatsfoot oil. Let's play catch, I said. I was running faster than ever in my PF Flyers. *Let's play catch*, I said, nearly singing it, and my father turned and said, *Let's not and say we did.*

The Seeded Light

Not quite evening, the fading light seeded with pollen. A white dog drinks water from its owner's hands next to a row of blue hydrangeas. They remind me of a planet I read about where it's always raining glass.

In Romania, a mother may have burned some masterpieces to save her son from prison. We will all be bits of nail and ash someday, like the evidence in her oven. The detritus of kings could be swirling in that light as well.

I try not to cling to the bodies I love, those vessels with faces and names in this place of lonely dust. The sun we used to worship wants us dead. What else can be expected when romance runs its course?

Only a child could love tonight, and one comes running up the street. The white dog ignores a stern command.

Basement Tapes

We bloomed radiant habits amid failed resurrections. Just one spark of light, though not satori brilliance. We were neon-less, nicotine-fingered. A warped disc spun on the turntable like a roulette wheel. We closed the door, turned inward wildly, tin foil smudged with tongue prints and blood on the cutting board. We felt the loud guitar, the primal guttural, the female vowels of mourning. When the burn subsided, we looked out the window at the bleached-out rag of sky, luminous behind stark branches. Dramatic shadings appeared, as if birds had flown past without their bodies. We closed our eyes, suddenly very tired, like ones who had wandered too far into the welcoming forest, unprepared for the cold night of everything.

THE CAPTAIN OF NO TEAM THAT I KNOW OF

For Denis Johnson

Outside The Last Resort, red pools of neon the rain made steam exotically and equatorially, and it would not be a surprise if some brightly feathered thing were to burst from a tree, squawking its head off, pinwheeling across the sky. But there is only the jukebox in the corner, spaceship blue with spinning lights, leaned on by a rail-thin woman in stone-washed jeans, who is clearly divorced from someone or something, and as you watch her close her eyes and sway, you envy her abandon, and you sip from your drink to quench your thirst, like thirst on Mercury.

A Green Ocean Somewhere Far Away

This is a rare occurrence, this intimacy, a funny thing, as in the eyes see the world askew. The retention pond wanes, a victim of the drought, like a moon that could never break away. I have just now noticed the stale air, the wisdom of loss I try not to enter. But there are feelings of love inside me that gnaw like small, burrowing creatures, a festival of them, who want nothing more than to reach the surface. Will someone be there, waiting, when they breach, when the spectacle demands an audience, and the known world seems far away? Probably not. The rain falls up to the sky. A sudden brightness makes the shade.

I Have Approximated Lightning

There is the ghost and then the ghost's shadow. By ghost, I mean memory. By shadow, I mean nothing. Or God. Or feral animals. I could mean father or mother, but I have decided that ghosts are preferable to parents, that feral animals are preferable to absent gods.

I grin to show my fear. The centuries of blood flow through me, a necessary poison. I mean only that this has been a long winter, cold, and full of snow that accumulates at night, that stuns the eyes in sunlight. I mean that I have approximated lightning in my heart and sensed the storm that follows.

And I have seen the pyramids made of diamonds and coal in the dream of nowhere left to go. They were beautiful and dangerous, and when I turned to you to say we should leave, you did.

Like IHOP at 3 A.M., I Radiate

Some nights, a half-century of longing crystallizes under my skin, and I want everything animal in me to rise up and howl. I want the discount liquors, the buy one get one free, the lucky numbers.

Like IHOP at 3 A.M., I radiate. Like the soft hair of death, my love is automatic. I echo the murders that appear on TV, unsolved and brutal. Clouds, thick and gray, accumulate until the sky resembles a slab of concrete, the world a mausoleum. I lurk without even trying, alive, for now, parading myself across the parking lot, alarming the shoppers who search for their cars among the many lookalikes.

I know the new meat is dry and flavorless. I know the mastodon would like to stay frozen, please. The dead, in dreams that last a millisecond, have visited me. They tell me everything matters or nothing does.

At any given moment, thousands of us are lying on our backs, receiving a transfusion. All those tubes and IV bags, streaming with the platelets of total strangers. Shouldn't it always be that way? Each of us aspiring to the heroic, flawed, then redeemed, an inspiration?

I want to embrace the concept of human kindness, but I don't know how much it costs. I do what I can to ease the worries.

When I speak to a child, I tell her no one really dies and mean it. Her face shines like flashes of light from a hundred Oppenheimer experiments. I mean no harm. There is no such thing as the soft hair of death.

CITY OF SHELLS

I spend a lot of time removing shells from living things. Sleep means things are quiet. I can hear it. The things with shells look like what I imagined a monster would be before I knew all monsters live inside me. It has been a long time since sleep.

In one corner of the room, a pile of shells nearly reaches the ceiling. It is a village of empty husks. A sculpture of useless carapaces; I would sleep inside one if I could.

I remove more shells. I don't remember when this began. It isn't likely to end. The city remains empty. The shells slide off with one shuck. I'm good at this. In another corner, a confusion of meat that walks.

FACTOTUM

Shame is the shotgun in the closet you hope no one ever finds. The rent will always be late. The sun will always seem distant and cruel. What are the odds that a fantastic one could ever lose to an ordinary asshole? Good, you think. The fantastic ones are always losing, mistaken for ordinary assholes, and the ordinary assholes are preening about disguised as the fantastic ones. This is the only explanation.

Whosoever decides that ending up with nothing is worth the risk of twice what is in the pocket already must agree the gods favor loss and still step up and roll the dice, scratch off the ticket's silver veil.

And you will wake before dawn to grunt through the streets, in galvanized and corrugated metal, evidence of drudge and epiphany, while the ones you love are still dreaming.

ORIENT

You float down a stream, passing towns and harbors. One day, you step out of the stream to look at something on the shore, a movement in the trees, a flash of light. There is nothing there, just the wind, or the sun's reflection on the leaves. When you turn to head back to the stream it is no longer apparent. You stand on what would be the shore if there were water at its border.

After a while you build a house, raise a family, and you stop looking for the stream. Many years pass, and one day you turn to see if the stream is there. It is not, as you suspected.

When you turn to head back to your house and family, they are no longer where you left them. In their place is a movement in the trees, a spark. You understand this to be nothing. You are standing in a place you know well, but it is different, neither stream nor shore. You ask yourself some questions, trying to remember a way back, but the questions outlive your attempt to find the answers.

That you cannot re-enter the stream, that you cannot find your house, of that there is no question.

Speculation About the Future

If I stand still long enough, I can feel my skin turn to bone. There's a clarity to my thoughts. The wind feels like silk against my body. I know that from a distance, I must resemble a statue, but I'm not made of stone. I am more like a shadow, a long, solitary shadow in a painting by de Chirico. Or like the sensation of walking down the street in one of those paintings, as if entering a new century or exploring a different planet. It's impossible to know if it's better to encounter what lives there or to be left completely alone. Now that I've been standing here forever, a little girl rolls a hoop along the street. Two men shake hands in the town square. Smoke issues from a train in the distance. I'm a shadow, dreaming of its body in the middle of it all. A giant clock, looming over the claustrophobic landscape, refuses to move its hands. I tell time by my own diminishing, by the sun's place in the sky, rising higher, arcing toward noon.

BIG MONEY FOR BROKEN GOLD

You pick away at the cross-hatched scars that cover you like palimpsests of every wrong desire. The map of tiny blue veins they cross seems faded as you gather your broken chains to pawn, measuring what counts weighed against the dross. It all reverts to sadness, gets boiled down, but never will you get what it's worth.

The sign outside the pawnshop reads: Big Money for Broken Gold. You sweep your tongue across the back of your teeth, the point probing each familiar crevice, hopeful about what still remains.

Like Any Other Planet

I knew your zip code. I saw Austin and I liked it. I stood outside the 7-11, shirtless, drinking alone. I could go as far as any other man, though my conveyances were limited to public means of transportation. Sometimes it was light and sometimes it was dark. You know, good days, bad days.

I saw the desert through the window of a Greyhound bus. It looked like any other planet where pain is the only feeling, but there were cacti blooming some kind of flower that may have been pink. Do you believe me?

I slept on and off in my seat, my head full of petrified spiders. I opened a book to make an impression, but no one took a glance. The seat beside me was always empty. The driver never stopped. I always thought he was headed your way.

Like Galileo

In the sleepless pilgrimage of every fucking night, I'm in my room, practicing my heresies on the points of dagger-jagged stars.

I know the physics. Here, then gone. Nothing is made of everything that used to be. Absence weighs more than a horse. And every discovery rockets us until we're further away.

It doesn't matter if I don't believe in ghosts, if ghosts believe in me. The scene of the crime is wherever I want it to be.

THE GRAND KINETIC NEON MACABRE

Before anyone was born, I attended the one and only Grand Kinetic Neon Macabre. I held a glow stick and talked for hours to the bathroom mirror. When someone asked me my name, I said I think it might rhyme with heaven. I said we could be radiant, if someone would dim the sun and spill some stardust on our skin.

But I'm tired of waiting, and tonight I want to start the Malibu with a screwdriver and caravan down to the careless side of town where they've captured pink light in glass tubes outside the girlie shows, which no one calls them anymore. Waste beds, green and glowing, will light the way.

This is America, turn of the century, and I have one foot in the previous century's grave. Set your phone to stun and beam me the fuck out of here. You know what I mean. I can't glow in the dark without thinking it should be dangerous.

SOME OTHER SPECIES OF LOVE

I walk the perimeter of my living room like the expectant father of a deformed child. I want to wrap myself in yellow crime scene tape and imitate an unsolved murder. I've developed sympathy for antipathy, the thought of gun ownership. My blood desires cool, damp air. My eyes seek to trade places with two black holes, to become a different kind of receptor.

When I look out the window, I see a semi's headlights threaded through the trees. Clouds hang as limp as beached jellyfish. The stars have burned themselves out. The luminous moon is strangely reminiscent. My soul is a memory locked tight in a black box at the bottom of the sea.

I would very much like to find myself among those stars, distant, dead, and gaze upon the planets of some other species of love. But tonight, a monster flexes up from inside me. It wears me like a cocoon. Ladies and gentlemen, the dormant period is over. It has wings. And twenty-four hours to live.

My Strategy

Like a song you love, this life is short and better because of it.

My strategy: remain small, walk the streets invisibly, wave goodbye before anyone knows I was here.

Once I saw a shrunken human head, eyes and lips sewn shut, face as smooth as an acorn, and wondered where its soul was.

My soul hides in the cabinet like a spider in a spaceship.

Exiled president of the hunger moon, I'm a light year away from my return.

READING CELAN ON LABOR DAY

Beneath the veil of this whitewashed, sun-fucked sky, it's hard to see. The dirty ragweed lays its yellow head on the parched grass. The neighbors carry their little bags of shit around the block.

Bees circle the reddening bushes like helicopters in a distant, hopeless war. The birch tree's black knobs blink like almond-shaped eyes. I narrow my cynical American eyes to decipher the words of a man who drowned on black milk.

The word for death is death.

COW HILL, BULL HILL

It's not the tedium of cold rain or the cliché of its presence. It's not the atmospheric conditions or the confluence of lakes when the glaciers moved through here eons ago, the slow, reticulating gesture of nature, mindless creator and destroyer. It's the certainty of mood, the gray of the interior life reflecting the sky that render me here, like a snapshot of myself, a still image in the charcoal wash where I float like a cloud of steam, amorphously, the air around me winter-midnight cold, and I'm amazed at the notion of my own consciousness and distill into the gradually warming air as the winter-heavy sun starts to filter down its silver light, where a few tall pines still feather the hills.

DEATH METAL SUNSET

All day I waited in the distance, collecting daylight like a sleeping cat. I have aged without wisdom. If bees didn't sting, I would love them. So many things God got wrong. The wind braids the long grasses where the doe and her fawn are dying. They breathe lavender and rain in their dreams of open fields. Sunset covers me in blood. Satan smokes me like a cigarette. I've rejected the mute insistence of trees. I need to sleep in the still warm belly of the stricken deer. There can be no other way tonight. I'm speaking a foreign language to the sickle moon. Apparently, the earth is never still, and I'm not the only one afraid of falling off. Look, a lonely sparrow going crazy in the dust. Now keeps happening.

Mourning, Not Rending

I hear music without wires and voices of the dead singing love songs from fifty years ago, and no one calls this a miracle, but I think it is, and so is the sun in the sky when the dead are still sleeping, and the clocks go on telling time though the dead take no notice, though I have seen crows mourn another crow on the street where I used to live, the street rain-soaked and dotted with samaras, and the crows crying out a human cry of disbelief, and in the air a murder flying in to see this, and at first I thought they were tearing at its flesh, but their cries implied otherwise, and I saw that they were mourning, not rending, and if blood needs to be shed it will be shed, and the bombed-out husks of buildings on the other side of the world are like stalagmites in a misty cave, and the guardian angels are beside themselves with grief and shame, the tiny white coffins an obscenity in the desert, this holy place where death makes more sense every day, all of it miraculous, all of it terrible, and the crows not moving when the wheel of my car approached.

ABOVE THE ASHES

You stayed above the ashes and watched from the bridge. Watched the small boats ply the still, blue waters while you pricked the skin of your thigh and slid the needle under. A cluster of stars behind your eyes. A flash of white. You carried yourself above the water and glided like a hawk across the phosphorescent sky.

When they found you, pulled to the side of the road, burned and half-decayed, it was because someone missed you enough to look. There is a word for this, but it must be in another language. Icarus of smack, someone called you father.

Like a Dog Barking at a Statue of the Virgin Mary

We are made of mayflies, of speech, an animal music, conscious of being and non-being, woven out of clouds or constellations, waiting to form memories, where we live forever with the dead in a jailed silence, among the human but apart, a strange kinship, translated to something like a dog barking at a statue of the Virgin Mary, or a bird confused by clear glass.

THE NATURAL WORLD

There is a sheen in the air like light through a jar of honey—dust mites filter through, striated, eight-legged. The rest of the world remains similarly odd. Outside, the Japanese maple loses its bark. Mold pocks the walkway. It's hard to breathe. Yellow pollen silts the lungs' mucus-soaked cells. A black snake undulates across the mulch. A blue jay bursts from the white birch. The chemical sunset spreads its human, inhuman beauty across the landscape. Starlings lose their minds. Corn stalks wither and bend. A blue heron flies, prehistorically, across the slate gray sky, determined to remind us.

Like a Werewolf on the Moon

To bluff is to be alive. I romance images because a thing once removed is easier to love. I pause but cannot pause you. Like Weldon Kees, sitting on a newspaper, I, too, look off in the distance, askew and aslant, my jazz pants fluttering. I drive bamboozled for hours in the already here and gone, until I feel like an old ship returning to port, then rain like nails on the roof, spores from black mold, a dull ache in my temple. As the beautiful woman once wrote about a beautiful woman: someone is tired of her. It deepens. My lunatic hours increase. Like a werewolf on the moon, I can't help it. Loneliness is another word for the music we've sent hurtling into space in the hope it will reach another civilization. That's how far away we are. We need rocket ships to send our love. It takes forever to get there. And no one speaks the language anyway.

THE GHOST

In the nether-morning, my ears shift from the industry of flies to the hum of sleek machines outside the window. I feel the bulwark of snow against the house and see the insistent swirling that sculpts the drifts and valleys.

I wonder how much torque it takes for wind to twist the way it does today. I think of the desert where you died, a whirl of sand, the miles between us turned to years, *brother* a foreign word for stranger.

What's not here, or, is here but invisible, silent, is like an animal in the woods at night, as afraid of you as you are of it, if it's even here at all.

(I know only as much as you did.)

The nearby lake is frozen. Catfish look at the stars through an endless sheet of ice.

You were always a thousand miles away.

Aegis in Abstentia

All the particulars have formed, all the accumulating carbon atoms that sought each other out in the wake of exploding stars to create what is human, now solidly headed toward the origins of decay.

All of it leading to this moment, your hands surrounding a cup of hot coffee in the fifties luncheonette, oldies spinning on the speckled blue jukebox, and the realization of flesh, fading toward fragile bone, like the blood rush of the spacewalk astronaut become untethered, the irrevocable moment that begs forgiveness that cannot be attained.

You ask the ether for a spoon, pour sugar from the glass dispenser on to the black Formica and try and try to read the signs, the constellations the granules form, your own night sky.

The waitress, eyeing the mess you've made, seems less and less intrigued by your musings, and you're loath to explain to her again the seriousness of your mission, the importance of which to her must seem like just another random spill.

THE BEAUTIFUL ZOO WHERE NO ONE SAYS I LOVE YOU

We are all prey here. Soft-bellied and slow. But at night we dream we are leopards and stalk the stars. It's a beautiful zoo, but there's no one here to say I love you. We all pray to be delivered but delivered from what we wonder.

And then the moon burns like an orange ember, and one of us goes mad and believes the dream, chases his tail in his sleep, devours it, disappears in front of our star-stunned eyes.

THESE THOUGHTS OF EXISTENCE

Completely apparent tonight, as surreptitious as a flock of anvils, these thoughts of existence assaulting us as the universe catapults toward oblivion. We're all practicing to be something inert, clownish, ready to take a last ride on a conveyer belt into the insatiable mouth of a crematorium's furnace or a tricked out hearse. In the meantime: endless displays of pastel confections, the spokesmodels' predatory white teeth, exclusive offers. I have nothing to offer except a tame resistance born of fear and an outmoded sense of justice. To clarify, I mean to die laughing, hopeless, in a good way.

Halloween

I felt doomed by starlight, by the bright exterior of the all-night diner, as if all light were predatory, obsessed with its ability to surge, to set something on fire. I felt like a statue trapped in a man's body. Or more like the shadow of a statue, a thing once removed from a thing. In the parking lot, there was an opening in the chain-link fence, a portal, a way in to the woods. The trees were suicidal with color. The leaves were trembling, expecting to fall. The sky was bleeding red at the wrist of horizon. Striated clouds scrimmed the moon. Past the trees, the steel mill's bright orange nocturnal glow. Sparks. A few silhouettes. The future. The past. I could feel my bones calcifying, my skull growing twice its size. A few children wearing creepy masks walked by. *We're monsters,* one of them shouted. *What are you?*

The Chaos Each Night Brings

I'm outside acknowledging the stars again, like a primitive being in search of gods with no knowledge that he is human—a forest dweller, a worshipper of fire in all its recent forms. I make sense of chaos to keep the blackness from being everything. There are no gods, but there are stories of gods. There is no such thing as love, and yet we love. Our story begins with an explosion. Our story ends differently for each of us. Particles of dust pretending to be mountains. Why do we keep talking about going into space when we're already there? The abducted girl escaped, but the kidnappers remain on the loose. I remember sleeping on the grass, a recursive breeze, the feeling I would never die. I didn't know the stars that shined were already dead. Some days I feel like that girl. Some days I feel like her abductors. But mostly I feel like a good cop, riding back to the station, trying to understand the deep sadness that finds him every time a case is closed.

CHRYSALIS

I used to fear sunset so much I'd hide in the corner of the living room and moan like a feral animal until it was dark, an infinite darkness like the womb, and I would sleep until first light, my Darvon/Valium wake-up call. I embraced disrepair and called a friend to hear another human voice but often wept at the sound, its temporary qualities. I could watch a fly climb a wall for hours until I remembered it had wings. A feeling as terrifying as church. I heard music in a minor key that made me think of horses and how they were once wild, and I felt afraid of my body. I could sleep all day and then not sleep at all, like a widow who has never lived alone, who says a prayer each hour to make the day go faster, as if prayer could raise the dead or calm the living, and I would not move for hours or answer when someone spoke, and I felt the peace of knowing I was both dead and alive. It wasn't my job to explain to anyone what that meant, and one day when I finally walked outside and looked down at the sidewalk, I saw a line of black ants carrying crumbs to their nest and decided it wouldn't hurt to keep on going.

SUSTAINABILITY

Nothing to eat except the same flora and fauna, brightly packaged, colorful, like a clown's face, and you have to choose, read the ingredients, set the time. Outside, querulous birdsong. Diesels struggling up the hill beneath a colorless sky. Voices that have been stilled were once recorded, and you listen to them to say, today, right now, fuck you, to death. What those birds are singing must mean something to them. You're thinking about mountains under water and wondering about those fish without eyes at the bottom of the ocean. There's no light and nothing to see. The timer rings. Not nothing. There's never nothing. You pull back the plastic and eat.

Searching for Terry Melcher

For John Coon

We had dreams that took us to L.A. on the cheap in a Valium stupor with Zory Zenith of Zolar X and the working poor. We may have lost a few to the slot machines in Reno, but the runaway from Wisconsin stayed poised in her seat, looming over us as she asked *Where are we?* every fifteen minutes, a question that began to take on an existential quality in Wyoming.

You do not know the land of the free if you haven't outrun a tornado across the whole of Nebraska as we have done. Are you experienced? We were, but not in a good way. We spent all we had on a shot and a beer in the St. Louis station. We took a leap of faith that ended in the Magic Hotel in West Hollywood with Bobby Whatshisname, sitting on his balcony above the pool, as if Nathaniel West had written him there.

What were we expecting from a rock and roll guru when we had no talent to speak of except our youth? Oh, Elvis is Jesus spelled American. They nailed him to a cross to keep his hips from shaking.

There Is a Word I Keep Forgetting

For Michael Burkard

This started as a forest and a pitcher of blue milk.

You found the door we walked through the night the moon appeared like a pink shell over Houston Street.

Door whisperer.

In the room we entered, we learned that a living man is scarier than his ghost.
It was as if we were inside the moon.

The moon was a pink shell, but I couldn't hear the sea. I heard the migraine pulsing of my heart, a thumping instead of.

Somewhere in the forest, a Buddhist temple appeared like a line from Coleridge.
You thought maybe your old phonograph was somewhere in an antique shop on Route 9.

My dream was of fire and yours was of Elvis, still alive.

I remember your father at the toy piano, touching the white keys and smiling.

There wasn't enough sunlight, so we said it was night.

My dream had fire, so we traded.

A pitcher of blue milk to douse the flames.

You showed me your ventriloquist doll, and I picked some books from your shelf and smelled the mold on them.

Your mother stayed in her room, as if she were a ghost.
I believed in her.
I believe in you, too.

There is a word I keep forgetting. I want to say it starts with D.
I know you would know if you were here. Are you here?
So many ghosts. So many of us hidden in our rooms.

I am losing more words, I suppose. You gave me many of them.
The dreams were a poor exchange.

We still have the mole people, though. The strange mark on the
father's neck.
And Baron Damone. Mr. Trolley. The Play Lady. Bob and Ray.

We did not ride a donkey there, but there was *something Don Quixote*
about it all.

You drew a colorful car and gave it to me. It had a childhood feel,
bright green and yellow.

You gave me Yesenin. Then you gave me Yesenin again.

You took one back, and now we both sleep with the rope's constant
threat.

I remember the funeral in your hometown, all of high school lined
up to say good-bye.

I would like to ride a donkey with you some day and take another
journey.

You can send me to the store again. I'll know the way this time.
There is a good chance I will return.

I will give you: the change, the way home, the hidden kitchen where you stood, while I looked the other way.

I will tell you my troubles like a blues man. There will be no shame.

I will establish a rhythm and a way of telling it. I will reach down to the depths and say what it is that keeps me awake and wakes me up when I sleep.

I will hum the melody and stamp my foot. My voice will deepen like the ocean.
My troubles will be ancient and holy.

We will sing to each other over the phone lines.
We will be like two hermit crabs that have buried themselves
in the terrarium's pink stones
and surface at exactly the same time on either end of their glass world.

And you will spin the blues back at me like a painting lost in the attic, lost, in fact, in the day that is this day, the voice that is your voice.

This could be the longest whispered childhood on record.

Algorithm

The past is black and white footage. A religion of dirt practiced in the dark. The tomb-shout echoing in the skull-bell. A priesthood made of knives. Your grandfather clanging shut a jail cell door, photographing a murder scene. The ruins of small boats, the oily gears of old clocks spread out on a card table. The long hallway attached to nothing, pitch black, like the entrance to a funhouse. On the wall: a head skewered by thorns, the Holy Ghost with its tongue of fire. Willows at the windows, crashing their limbs like grieving widows, the wind's howl the only syllable, the only prayer, like the shriek of an exotic bird stolen from an intricate cage. Always night. Always the lights, just about to come on.

NORTH ISLAND
For Bei Dao

You could be from anywhere but never go home. For you, all cities were ruins; every room four corners of foreign, the bed's white sheet a blank passport to bad dreams.

I wished you were a bird, so you could fly over the globe's perfect grid and land on a strong branch.

> The world is very small now.

I don't need to give you the wings I made for you from burning leaves. I'm not saying goodbye. I'm writing to ask, where are you, now that home is the head of a pin?

GRAVEYARD, ROOT, AND FOREST

I cut through the graveyard in the dark on the way home from the movie that wouldn't end. Past all the grandmother houses swollen with foreign vowels.

There are actually two forests . . . one at the end of the other.

The owl's cadence notwithstanding, I walked as if unafraid. The leaf-grim trees above and below—another eerie silence.

I have dreamt of the great taproot that pierced your heart. I am driven and driven toward your grave, dissatisfied. Here is the latest vehicle: an ice wagon filled with bones.

Meet me where the roots begin to tangle.

To be a child is to look for a larger hand. Another science of the trees that grow above and beneath you.

Meet me where the earth meets a different earth.

IV

CLUES FROM THE ANIMAL KINGDOM

It seems you're here again, pitching the weight of the bruise you call
    a body against the world that eludes you.

Or is it the sky, ethereal, cloud-coffined, that bears down on you
    like a carnival at closing time, dimming of light

and echo of voices that must be the wind, lost in the sun-stroke hours,
    the blood-laced ferns.

Some species of spiders will eat their mothers when food is scarce.

What are we afraid of? Nothing specific, just the speed of light and
    sound, the usual concerns

that the bullet will hit before we hear the gunshot. That's how we pass
    the summer, tuned

to the city's dangers in the shimmer and glow of whatever
    lurks in the distance.

Cows can sleep standing up but only dream when lying down.

I've seen you pretend to be a dinosaur and lumber across a dew-
    sopped lawn, terrifying yourself and others,

drunk on some potion you said you found. Mainly you slump, curl
    into a ball,

small enough to fit in a bottle, to captain the ship inside toward a
    future that doesn't contain you.

Ants never sleep.

If I ask, *Where are you going*, is there an answer? I expect you to mime
　　the pulling of a rope,

the shrinking of a box. A napalm shower, the rain explodes and fires up
　　your nerves.

Keep in mind as you look at the sky for signs of meteors,
　　the dinosaurs had no choice.

A cobra can bite as soon as it is born.

I know I need to make this clearer, to bridge the gap between fact
　　and fiction, between earth and outer space.

I know the space between us is greater than the distance
　　between snow and fire.

I know it would take a metaphysician to rearrange our molecules,
　　make gold from the lead our lives have become.

A drop of alcohol will make a scorpion go crazy and sting itself to death.

I'm saying, don't go; don't escape from the neighborhood of love
　　you're convinced burned down.

Should I admit I'm talking to myself again, as it is when I pray?
　　It is as it has always been.

Flies always buzz in the key of F.

What I learned from the mosquito: the one that hums is not the one
　　that takes your blood.

MONSTROUS

Unusual sounds in the air tonight—a mix of screams and animal laughter, as if everything we ever thought was chasing us has finally tracked us down. In the sky, stars like bits of broken glass stuck in warm asphalt after a terrible accident.

I understand we are indistinguishable from any other paired and desperate creatures. I realize we are flummoxed by our need to sear each other's wounds, that we can never stop the accident of every night from happening.

But here they are, the monsters we thought we'd always keep at bay, surrounding the house, crashing through windows and doors, chanting our names, determined to give us exactly what we want.

Zen Portraiture

A house faces north all day long. North faces south. Southern light floods the windows and makes rectangles on the floor. They see this every day but never notice. House with bright green painting. House with photos of calcified sand. The air cools at night. They pull the blanket to their chins. They sense the bulwark of snow against the windows. Deer scat in the morning. Drops of blood in the snow. Her face as small as lemons. His face widening in the mirror. Row of sumacs. Dearth of panicles. *What did you say? Nothing.* How to begin the day as the neighbor's dog barks insistently. A white spider climbs the headboard. White of old snow. White of chipped porcelain. Towels hang in the bathroom like discouraged ghosts. The world in their heads fabricates the world they're given. There is a word for everything. Her hair is not a color. His skin collapses. They only notice the geese as they are leaving. A photograph of a window. A painting of the sea. They can hear the blue in the painting letting go, the music of its departure changing chords from major to minor. They're on a ship that glides along the blue wave. If you look at them through the clear vase filled with water, they appear to be drowning.

At Brooklyn Pickle

I have issues with the sandwich place. Sun through plate glass like a golden blade. Bone cold loneliness of meat. Customers appearing to be more stable than they are, as if they couldn't suddenly be sucked up into the air. I wait for my sandwich, while a man with a face like a sheet of gray ice checks scores on his phone as his grandchildren roll across the mud-stained floor in a failed attempt to be noticed. Will no one stand up and scream, release the unbearable tension we all must be feeling? I can see on every face the desire for the ceiling to collapse, or the gunman to enter, weapon drawn, his mind a tangle of snakes, the longing for a small catastrophe to put an end to it all. At the end of the world, it will be just like this, a lethargy disguising the boiled nerves of the last humans at their feeding. The sandwich arrives. I unwrap and savor. Think it's strange but necessary. Tear off a fringe of ham. I held a pig, once, and felt its beating heart.

MARITAL

The room reeks of spoiled chicken. The letters on TV are neon pink. Color of flamingoes if flamingoes glowed in the dark. The actress's tattoos are the skyline of a city we may have visited. I can't tell if they're dancing or walking. It's all halfway. But there's music, the kind I imagine we would dance to if we were different people. This is beginning to look familiar. This is beginning to look interesting. This is the scene we watched in Spanish.

Sinkhole in Knife Town

Without the very foundation on which I place my feet, or the illusion of permanence that lets me sleep, briefly, I might as well surrender. But I go on like the geese that woke me with their loud departure in pearl-gray skies, and occasionally, a gunshot, and still they wouldn't abort their flight, and now there's a sinkhole in Knife Town, one more reason to go back to sleep.

But I forge on like an ant toward sugar, a crooked line of insatiable desires. And if the bottom drops out, so be it, no need to dig a grave or wallow doom and gloom-style in righteous indignation, cursing the sky for not being heaven, convinced that sinkhole is another word for hell.

ORANGE SUNSHINE

We are not dancing. We are standing near the kitchen sink, pouring water from a vase, watching the burnt pink petals of the flowers, like the delicate folds of skin that cover the eyes of wild horses, swirling down the drain, and I remember a lifetime ago, looking at my face in the mirror, stunned there, as my temple's snake vein pulsed and bloomed, stupid as a blue rose.

Quarantine

I grieve the hours we spent in a shadow-strewn room where silk scarves dangled from the bedposts, and I launched my body against yours in an amphetamine frenzy, passionate and useless, as the basement filled with rain, and the smell of dampness told us our fate was mold, our future toxic, triggering the slow dissolve, the aperture reduction, the merciful fade into reason.

Now our bodies sleep apart as if quarantined on different ships, our fevers the same, their sources separate. Every moment is a trespass of the past, a circus of want in a barren wilderness of need, and though I will die this way in a cheap suit of regret and failure, I think of those abandoned hours with fondness, though our expressions were not the expressions of the creatures we wished to be, our animal hearts accelerating inside us, as we lay beneath the bone-white seriousness of the moon.

In the Realm of Minor Keys

Everywhere the hummingbird wings beat death, and quarter notes ring in the ether like solos from a lost guitar. The shadows of enormous violet clouds lumber across the hills like Roman galleons . . . like migrating whales . . . like . . .

Grief is all the shadows I never notice until it's nightfall. There is only so much lightning in any storm. Everything dangerous sparks and disappears.

If your ghost were a shadow, it would follow me forever. If blue were not a color, it would taste like salt. If a piano were not an instrument, I would sail it home to you.

Don't you ever wonder what made the first humans sing?

Triptych: Analogy of Faith

Christ in Limbo

An angry Christ enters limbo with a cross held over his head like a spear. He's pushing open the door and appears to be crushing three demons made of burnished silver, one with bloody hands, crying out from its birdlike head. (Who guards the gates of limbo?) I see a wild thing with a funnel over its head, running away past some creatures who appear to be gambling at a baize-covered table. Elsewhere a flayed body hangs upside down near some severed limbs.

Outside my window, Canada geese lift skyward with their black and white heads held above the frantic beating of wings, the sky darkens, and a flickering shadow covers the lawn for a few moments.

The rest of the panel is a landscape of suffering that belies how I was told the unbaptized spend eternity. I had pictured a large room, empty except for unfortunate babies tended by pagans who had lived good lives, a kind of netherworld nursery where nothing ever happens.

Self Portrait

It's been said that Bosch placed his own face, placid, whitish gray, in the Hell panel of *The Garden of Earthly Delights*. It's what stands out to me, the stealthy calm inside the storm of tortured flesh, his head a ghostly Where's Waldo?, hidden in plain sight in the painting of the monsters in his head. In his head, a hell much worse than anyone had ever dreamed of, and his eyes, askance, as if he could see beyond the menagerie of tortured souls and his Prince of Hell to the Heaven panel, places I no longer bother to imagine.

I click the tab and it closes. The screen is black. It is black outside, too. I can see the blood moon out the window now, watching me, winking as in an old cartoon. The moon disappears behind a cloud as if eaten by one of Bosch's demons. I sit and wait for it to be expelled. The room shades dark as a confessional.

AGAINST SURREALISM

The human heart weighs ten ounces, but I don't know if it can float.

I don't suppose it makes sense to say I feel like the tail of Halley's comet, but what do you want from the truth?

The daylilies are silent, but no one accuses them of being shy. Mother, are all your memories being trampled by a stampede of wild horses?

I left the chicken in the pot so long it turned black. It's too late for an apology, but I can buy you a headstone to match your husband's. Though when the sun's too bright, it's hard to find the gravesite; then you can end up on the road to the old sanitarium.

I don't know if a human heart can float, but in my cage of bones last night mine beat like a hummingbird's wings.

The grass is yellow from the drought. Some plants are dead and others are thriving. The lakes stand shallow. The rivers run weak. I believe my heart would sink.

CAUSALITY

Here is the sequence as I understand it: asteroid, meteor, meteorite.

Transformation stories usually inspire me to imagine my own better self, but somehow the diminishing of a planet-like object to space debris is too much to bear. The religions of the world offer no solace. I am alone with my thoughts, again. Will high school ever end?

Sure, I think you're pretty. Everyone thinks you're pretty. But once I saw you laughing when I was feeling sad.

My Face Is a Stranger to the Mirror of God

The equation is simple: for there to be music, there must also be pain. As when the sheep is slaughtered, the gut is dried and stretched to make the strings that lay across the instrument.

At times, one can hear the sheep's cry when the bow scrapes softly against the lowest string. It is a kind of plea, the slain beast crying out to God, but going only so far as the human ear.

This is why we invented another world.

But my face is a stranger to the mirror of God; the bellows of night exhale all around me; something hidden in the trees blinks its yellow eyes.

Like an eye adjusting to the dark, I can see the shapes of things. I rise and walk slowly, arms extended, unsure, but willing to risk a false step, an injured foot.

Each step surer than the one before it, I make my way toward the door. Behind it could be bright light or simply more of the same ill-lit, barely navigable world.

I move step by step and breathe softly, as if I were the nighttime prayer of a frightened child, making my way toward heaven.

Autobiography of an Excised Heart

I was born a goldfish at the New York State Fair. I swam small circles inside a bag I thought was the world. When a giant hand released me into a glass aquarium, I saw other fish the color of Hindu gods. I hid inside a castle and watched as bubbles spewed from the mask of a miniature man who never moved.

At night, the sun burned out in an instant. I dreamed I could fly and breathe air. My fins were obscene vestiges. I fell back asleep to escape my shame. I grew plump and red with human blood.

When I woke, I was packed in ice inside a blue cooler, swimming toward the chest of an unfortunate man.

Historical

Nothing moves me further away toward a mathematical horizon, completely abstract, like an oarless boat on a perfectly still body of endless water, as when you speak to me in the fifty languages of nowhere. Though I have no answer, everything tastes like snow, a mineral sulk on the tongue, the essence of winter locked in every molecule. The woolly mammoth kissing his bride. A universe of ice embracing us. Everything beautiful and breathtaking. Almost wandering, we finally arrive. We build our nests that turn to stone. We make a wheel of fire. Then someone invents the word for bread; then horde; then empire. *Look at us*, we say. Then history begins.

At Least Our Ruins Will Be Spectacular

Will we be forever the bone of an idea but never the idea, never manifest or sacred, always more like something purchased at the convenience store after filling up, cheap and large, regrettable? Will we be broken as light is broken in water, refracted, a trick? Even in our sleep we can't forget. Stars eating stars. Blue water stippled with light. A shoebox full of teeth. A dog full of many other dogs. Our cells are being replaced by false cells, mechanical cells, until we are machines that resemble us. We can hear the werewolves singing. They're so sad, we forgive them all their mayhem. A statue laments a lost finger, weary of the chipped pedestal at its feet and the snow that falls like white spiders all around it. We trade our souls for expensive shoes. We hope at least our ruins will be spectacular: the loam of eyes from fallen saints, pianos floating on rough waters. The ocean in a shell on our doorsteps.

TIME TRAVEL

The red needle bobbed and sank on my way to see who you used to be. The car drifted, stalled. Through the windshield, the night sky loomed, parked like a truck with one bad headlight. I stepped out on the shoulder and shuffled backwards, serpentine, down the gorge road to town to get a dollar's worth, striking match against flint, hoping the wind would lose its desire. The animals of night began to scream; cold air translated rain to snow. The match flared; I took a drag. Emitting a weak signal of distress, my cigarette burned down to within an inch of its life. I was like a time traveler, stranded in my own past, driven to embrace you in a basement furnished with broken chairs, a man who knows and doesn't care that the future is a semi made of stars, careening through the massive, endless dark.

DRIFT AND SWAY

Rain worried the roof all night. I listened for mold to sprout in the basement. I waited for mushrooms to burst forth from the baseboards. I stayed still on the damp sheets so I wouldn't be torn by the mattress spring. I dreamed I gave you a bracelet strung with baby teeth and spiders. I promised myself I'd get up on the count of three, but I wanted to watch the movie I made up of you in the ultra-sunlight of July. You were framed there like a Hopper nude. I was like a dead jazz musician, watching his own funeral in New Orleans. I still don't know what kind of cat was prowling near the highway last night, but it was big with yellow eyes. Why everyone moves away I'll never understand. I will split your tongue with my kiss when you go. This is my last prayer: *Dear Lord, why is the moon my father?*

THE HIDDEN WISHES OF THE NIGHT

A yellow veil of pollen covered the known world. I felt the knife-slice of October, its carnival of leaves. I pretended the sound of my own name was meaningful. The red sun vanished and the clouds moved on, a poignancy that frightened me.

I heard an old crow sing the hidden wishes of the night, the genius mantra of the thief. I knew the way home is always the same, but home wasn't always there. I never questioned what was handed to me. I woke up often on the sharp edge of surrender to a paralyzing unholiness, the reverie of flies, the smoked-down cigarettes of the dead, and I listened to an urgent music that seemed trapped in amber, the random casino of the stars all there was to help me navigate.

I learned mind expansion was mind destruction and sat still for a few years, contemplating the Disneyland of my empty hands. I discovered the subliminal messages of the human heart by listening to my own and heard the pulse of a hummingbird on crystal meth. I ate the moon, because I was so hungry, so dead.

The story I was told that saved me is this: A man was buried alive, and when they dug up his grave and opened the coffin, his fingers were worn down to the nub.

Visit to a Random Orchard

This place is as good as any. The pageantry of stars gets old. But the vastness-closeness-farawayness never ends. Apple trees crouch like giant, sci-fi spiders. White petals blow away toward the granary.

I carry the disappointment of the old house key, the father-comb, the wedding ring with no diamonds. I feign a prayer I can't remember the words to.

In the distance, I see the lake at sunset flash like a knife. I open the shoebox and let all my mother's photographs scatter across the orchard.

Some of the photographs are black and white. Some are in the washed-out colors of the past. Some of the faces I know and some are strangers. Some of the faces I know are strangers, too.

THIS PHARAOH OF I

A snail lay with the spirit patient. Its dull progression left its trail, its body a map of where a body should not go. The spirit patient rose from sleep. He followed the trail. He began to understand his sickness. He marked the snail's progress as a way of understanding his life. From another room, he heard stories of men and women, of gods. He said to himself, I assume this pharaoh of I dwells also in the other world. He noticed, briefly, the snail crawling out of the room, oozing its way across the floor. It took forever; the spirit patient grew bored with eternity. He turned to watch a pigeon land on the windowsill, and he listened as the room filled with its cooing. The pigeon flew into the room and pinched the snail in its beak. All of time is divided into moments such as this one, thought the spirit patient. His sickness lifted. The pigeon perched on the windowsill again, the snail a small protrusion.

Acknowledgments

Grateful acknowledgment is made to the editors of the following print and on-line journals in which these poems first appeared, some in different versions:

Action, Spectacle: "Family Tree," "Triptych: Analogy of Faith";
Ampersand: "Big Money for Broken Gold," "The Captain of No Team That I Know of," "Monstrous";
The Bakery: "Postulate," "Radiant Fish," "Recidivist Rex";
Birdfeast: "How I Learned to Play Guitar";
Corresponding Voices: "North Island," "Orange Sunshine," "Visit to a Random Orchard";
dcomP magazinE: "Like a Werewolf on the Moon," "Marital," "The Natural World";
Flock: "Death Metal Sunset," "These Thoughts of Existence," "Zen Portraiture";
H_NGM_N: "Drift and Sway," "A Green Ocean Somewhere Far Away";
Heavy Feather Review: "A Better Theater Than My Skull," "City of Shells," "I Have Approximated Lightning";
Juked: "The Beautiful Zoo Where No One Says I Love You," "Five Fictions";
The Laurel Review: "The Grand Kinetic Neon Macabre," "Searching for Terry Melcher," "The Seeded Light," "Temporal Location Finder";
Miracle Monocle: "An Old-Fashioned Comedy," "Speculation About the Future";
NAATAN: "Autobiography of an Excised Heart";
New York Tyrant: "At Least Our Ruins Will Be Spectacular," "Basement Tapes," "Chrysalis," "Coaxing the Dog Inside," "Halloween," "Some Other Species of Love," "Scuola Metafisica," "Sustainability";
Nine Mile: "Algorithm," "The Ghost," "Like a Dog Barking at a Statue of the Virgin Mary," "Mourning, Not Rending,"

"There Is a Word I Keep Forgetting";

The Offending Adam: "Folk Tale," "Like Any Other Planet,"
   "Quarantine";

Ovenbird: "Between Heaven and Hell," "Reading Celan on Labor
   Day";

Ploughshares: "Historical";

Plume Anthology 5: "The Double Sedative";

Plume: "Against Surrealism," "Clues from the Animal Kingdom,"
   "Confusing Myself with the Whippoorwill";

Post Road: "At Brooklyn Pickle," "My Strategy";

The Weekly Rumpus: "Factotum," "Small Hope Factor," "Time
   Travel";

Wigleaf: "The Black Boot, the River, the Burning House," "In the
   Realm of Minor Keys," "Like Sailboats on TV";

Willows Wept Review: "Cow Hill, Bull Hill."

Some of these poems appear, some in slightly different form, in the chapbook, *Once I Saw You Laughing When I Was Feeling Sad*, published by Midnight City Books.

I would like to thank my editor, Peter Conners, for his attention to the various iterations of the manuscript that became this book and Ron Martin-Dent, Kelly Hatton, Richard Foerster, and Daphne Morrissey for all their input. Thanks also to Mi Ditmar, Sarah Harwell, and Corey Zeller for their editorial insights. Thanks to Gian DiTrapano, John Gallaher, Scott Garson, and Daniel Lawless for their support. Thanks to the faculty in the MFA Program at Syracuse University and to my current and former students for their constant inspiration. Thanks to the National Endowment for the Arts for the fellowship that afforded me time to work on these poems.

Special thanks to Tessa Kennedy for her fantastic collage and to Steph Scheirer for encouraging me when it made no sense to do so.

The Tomas Tranströmer quote is from *Memories Look at Me: A Memoir*, New Directions (2011): 37.

ABOUT THE AUTHOR

Christopher Kennedy is the author of *Ennui Prophet* (BOA Editions, Ltd.), *Encouragement for a Man Falling to His Death* (BOA Editions, Ltd.), which received the Isabella Gardner Poetry Award in 2007, *Trouble with the Machine* (Low Fidelity Press), and *Nietzsche's Horse* (Mitki/Mitki Press). He is one of the translators of *Light and Heavy Things: Selected Poems of Zeeshan Sahil*, (BOA Editions, Ltd.), published as part of the Lannan Translation Selection Series. His work has appeared in many print and online journals and magazines, including *Ploughshares, Plume, New York Tyrant, Ninth Letter, Wigleaf, The Threepenny Review, Mississippi Review,* and *McSweeney's*. In 2011, he was awarded an NEA Fellowship for Poetry. He is a professor of English at Syracuse University where he directs the MFA Program in Creative Writing.

BOA Editions, Ltd. American Poets Continuum Series

No. 1   *The Fuhrer Bunker: A Cycle of
         Poems in Progress*
         W. D. Snodgrass

No. 2   *She*
         M. L. Rosenthal

No. 3   *Living With Distance*
         Ralph J. Mills, Jr.

No. 4   *Not Just Any Death*
         Michael Waters

No. 5   *That Was Then: New and
         Selected Poems*
         Isabella Gardner

No. 6   *Things That Happen Where
         There Aren't Any People*
         William Stafford

No. 7   *The Bridge of Change:
         Poems 1974–1980*
         John Logan

No. 8   *Signatures*
         Joseph Stroud

No. 9   *People Live Here: Selected
         Poems 1949–1983*
         Louis Simpson

No. 10   *Yin*
         Carolyn Kizer

No. 11   *Duhamel: Ideas of Order in
         Little Canada*
         Bill Tremblay

No. 12   *Seeing It Was So*
         Anthony Piccione

No. 13   *Hyam Plutzik:
         The Collected Poems*

No. 14   *Good Woman: Poems and a
         Memoir 1969–1980*
         Lucille Clifton

No. 15   *Next: New Poems*
         Lucille Clifton

No. 16   *Roxa: Voices of the Culver
         Family*
         William B. Patrick

No. 17   *John Logan: The Collected Poems*

No. 18   *Isabella Gardner: The Collected
         Poems*

No. 19   *The Sunken Lightship*
         Peter Makuck

No. 20   *The City in Which I Love You*
         Li-Young Lee

No. 21   *Quilting: Poems 1987–1990*
         Lucille Clifton

No. 22   *John Logan: The Collected
         Fiction*

No. 23   *Shenandoah and Other Verse
         Plays*
         Delmore Schwartz

No. 24   *Nobody Lives on Arthur
         Godfrey Boulevard*
         Gerald Costanzo

No. 25   *The Book of Names:
         New and Selected Poems*
         Barton Sutter

No. 26   *Each in His Season*
         W. D. Snodgrass

No. 27   *Wordworks: Poems Selected
         and New*
         Richard Kostelanetz

No. 28   *What We Carry*
         Dorianne Laux

No. 29   *Red Suitcase*
         Naomi Shihab Nye

No. 30   *Song*
         Brigit Pegeen Kelly

No. 31   *The Fuehrer Bunker:
         The Complete Cycle*
         W. D. Snodgrass

No. 32   *For the Kingdom*
         Anthony Piccione

No. 33   *The Quicken Tree*
         Bill Knott

No. 34   *These Upraised Hands*
         William B. Patrick

No. 35   *Crazy Horse in Stillness*
         William Heyen

No. 36   *Quick, Now, Always*
          Mark Irwin

No. 37   *I Have Tasted the Apple*
          Mary Crow

No. 38   *The Terrible Stories*
          Lucille Clifton

No. 39   *The Heat of Arrivals*
          Ray Gonzalez

No. 40   *Jimmy & Rita*
          Kim Addonizio

No. 41   *Green Ash, Red Maple,*
          Black Gum
          Michael Waters

No. 42   *Against Distance*
          Peter Makuck

No. 43   *The Night Path*
          Laurie Kutchins

No. 44   *Radiography*
          Bruce Bond

No. 45   *At My Ease: Uncollected Poems*
          of the Fifties and Sixties
          David Ignatow

No. 46   *Trillium*
          Richard Foerster

No. 47   *Fuel*
          Naomi Shihab Nye

No. 48   *Gratitude*
          Sam Hamill

No. 49   *Diana, Charles, & the Queen*
          William Heyen

No. 50   *Plus Shipping*
          Bob Hicok

No. 51   *Cabato Sentora*
          Ray Gonzalez

No. 52   *We Didn't Come Here for This*
          William B. Patrick

No. 53   *The Vandals*
          Alan Michael Parker

No. 54   *To Get Here*
          Wendy Mnookin

No. 55   *Living Is What I Wanted:*
          Last Poems
          David Ignatow

No. 56   *Dusty Angel*
          Michael Blumenthal

No. 57   *The Tiger Iris*
          Joan Swift

No. 58   *White City*
          Mark Irwin

No. 59   *Laugh at the End of the World:*
          Collected Comic Poems 1969–
          1999
          Bill Knott

No. 60   *Blessing the Boats: New and*
          Selected Poems: 1988–2000
          Lucille Clifton

No. 61   *Tell Me*
          Kim Addonizio

No. 62   *Smoke*
          Dorianne Laux

No. 63   *Parthenopi: New and Selected*
          Poems
          Michael Waters

No. 64   *Rancho Notorious*
          Richard Garcia

No. 65   *Jam*
          Joe-Anne McLaughlin

No. 66   *A. Poulin, Jr. Selected Poems*
          Edited, with an Introduction
          by Michael Waters

No. 67   *Small Gods of Grief*
          Laure-Anne Bosselaar

No. 68   *Book of My Nights*
          Li-Young Lee

No. 69   *Tulip Farms and Leper Colonies*
          Charles Harper Webb

No. 70   *Double Going*
          Richard Foerster

No. 71   *What He Took*
          Wendy Mnookin

No. 72   *The Hawk Temple at Tierra*
          Grande
          Ray Gonzalez

No. 73   *Mules of Love*
          Ellen Bass

No. 74   *The Guests at the Gate*
          Anthony Piccione

No. 75   *Dumb Luck*
          Sam Hamill

No. 76 *Love Song with Motor Vehicles*
Alan Michael Parker

No. 77 *Life Watch*
Willis Barnstone

No. 78 *The Owner of the House: New Collected Poems 1940–2001*
Louis Simpson

No. 79 *Is*
Wayne Dodd

No. 80 *Late*
Cecilia Woloch

No. 81 *Precipitates*
Debra Kang Dean

No. 82 *The Orchard*
Brigit Pegeen Kelly

No. 83 *Bright Hunger*
Mark Irwin

No. 84 *Desire Lines: New and Selected Poems*
Lola Haskins

No. 85 *Curious Conduct*
Jeanne Marie Beaumont

No. 86 *Mercy*
Lucille Clifton

No. 87 *Model Homes*
Wayne Koestenbaum

No. 88 *Farewell to the Starlight in Whiskey*
Barton Sutter

No. 89 *Angels for the Burning*
David Mura

No. 90 *The Rooster's Wife*
Russell Edson

No. 91 *American Children*
Jim Simmerman

No. 92 *Postcards from the Interior*
Wyn Cooper

No. 93 *You & Yours*
Naomi Shihab Nye

No. 94 *Consideration of the Guitar: New and Selected Poems 1986–2005*
Ray Gonzalez

No. 95 *Off-Season in the Promised Land*
Peter Makuck

No. 96 *The Hoopoe's Crown*
Jacqueline Osherow

No. 97 *Not for Specialists: New and Selected Poems*
W. D. Snodgrass

No. 98 *Splendor*
Steve Kronen

No. 99 *Woman Crossing a Field*
Deena Linett

No. 100 *The Burning of Troy*
Richard Foerster

No. 101 *Darling Vulgarity*
Michael Waters

No. 102 *The Persistence of Objects*
Richard Garcia

No. 103 *Slope of the Child Everlasting*
Laurie Kutchins

No. 104 *Broken Hallelujahs*
Sean Thomas Dougherty

No. 105 *Peeping Tom's Cabin: Comic Verse 1928–2008*
X. J. Kennedy

No. 106 *Disclamor*
G.C. Waldrep

No. 107 *Encouragement for a Man Falling to His Death*
Christopher Kennedy

No. 108 *Sleeping with Houdini*
Nin Andrews

No. 109 *Nomina*
Karen Volkman

No. 110 *The Fortieth Day*
Kazim Ali

No. 111 *Elephants & Butterflies*
Alan Michael Parker

No. 112 *Voices*
Lucille Clifton

No. 113 *The Moon Makes Its Own Plea*
Wendy Mnookin

No. 114 *The Heaven-Sent Leaf*
Katy Lederer

No. 115 *Struggling Times*
Louis Simpson

No. 116 *And*
Michael Blumenthal

No. 117 *Carpathia*
Cecilia Woloch

No. 118 *Seasons of Lotus, Seasons of Bone*
Matthew Shenoda

No. 119 *Sharp Stars*
Sharon Bryan

No. 120 *Cool Auditor*
Ray Gonzalez

No. 121 *Long Lens: New and Selected Poems*
Peter Makuck

No. 122 *Chaos Is the New Calm*
Wyn Cooper

No. 123 *Diwata*
Barbara Jane Reyes

No. 124 *Burning of the Three Fires*
Jeanne Marie Beaumont

No. 125 *Sasha Sings the Laundry on the Line*
Sean Thomas Dougherty

No. 126 *Your Father on the Train of Ghosts*
G.C. Waldrep and John Gallaher

No. 127 *Ennui Prophet*
Christopher Kennedy

No. 128 *Transfer*
Naomi Shihab Nye

No. 129 *Gospel Night*
Michael Waters

No. 130 *The Hands of Strangers: Poems from the Nursing Home*
Janice N. Harrington

No. 131 *Kingdom Animalia*
Aracelis Girmay

No. 132 *True Faith*
Ira Sadoff

No. 133 *The Reindeer Camps and Other Poems*
Barton Sutter

No. 134 *The Collected Poems of Lucille Clifton: 1965–2010*

No. 135 *To Keep Love Blurry*
Craig Morgan Teicher

No. 136 *Theophobia*
Bruce Beasley

No. 137 *Refuge*
Adrie Kusserow

No. 138 *The Book of Goodbyes*
Jillian Weise

No. 139 *Birth Marks*
Jim Daniels

No. 140 *No Need of Sympathy*
Fleda Brown

No. 141 *There's a Box in the Garage You Can Beat with a Stick*
Michael Teig

No. 142 *The Keys to the Jail*
Keetje Kuipers

No. 143 *All You Ask for Is Longing: New and Selected Poems 1994–2014*
Sean Thomas Dougherty

No. 144 *Copia*
Erika Meitner

No. 145 *The Chair: Prose Poems*
Richard Garcia

No. 146 *In a Landscape*
John Gallaher

No. 147 *Fanny Says*
Nickole Brown

No. 148 *Why God Is a Woman*
Nin Andrews

No. 149 *Testament*
G.C. Waldrep

No. 150 *I'm No Longer Troubled by the Extravagance*
Rick Bursky

No. 151 *Antidote for Night*
Marsha de la O

No. 152 *Beautiful Wall*
Ray Gonzalez

No. 153 *the black maria*
Aracelis Girmay

No. 154 *Celestial Joyride*
Michael Waters

No. 155 *Whereso*
Karen Volkman

No. 156 *The Day's Last Light Reddens the Leaves of the Copper Beech*
Stephen Dobyns

No. 157 *The End of Pink*
Kathryn Nuernberger

No. 158 *Mandatory Evacuation*
Peter Makuck

No. 159 *Primitive: The Art and Life of Horace H. Pippin*
Janice N. Harrington

No. 160 *The Trembling Answers*
Craig Morgan Teicher

No. 161 *Bye-Bye Land*
Christian Barter

No. 162 *Sky Country*
Christine Kitano

No. 163 *All Soul Parts Returned*
Bruce Beasley

No. 164 *The Smoke of Horses*
Charles Rafferty

No. 165 *The Second O of Sorrow*
Sean Thomas Dougherty

No. 166 *Holy Moly Carry Me*
Erika Meitner

No. 167 *Clues from the Animal Kingdom*
Christopher Kennedy

COLOPHON

BOA Editions, Ltd., a not-for-profit publisher of poetry and other literary works, fosters readership and appreciation of contemporary literature. By identifying, cultivating, and publishing both new and established poets and selecting authors of unique literary talent, BOA brings high-quality literature to the public. Support for this effort comes from the sale of its publications, grant funding, and private donations.

☙❧

The publication of this book is made possible, in part,
by the support of the following individuals:

Anonymous
Angela Bonazinga & Catherine Lewis
Gwen & Gary Conners
Gouvernet Arts Fund
Sandi Henschel, *in honor of Lisa Richele Piccione*
and Juan Antonio Garcia
Jack & Gail Langerak
Susan Burke & William Leonardi, *in honor of Boo Poulin*
Melanie & Ron Martin-Dent
Edith Matthai, *in memory of Peter Hursh*
Joe McElveney
Dan Meyers, *in honor of J. Shepard Skiff*
Steve & Theo Munson
Boo Poulin
Deborah Ronnen & Sherman Levey
Steven O. Russell & Phyllis Rifkin-Russell
Allan & Melanie Ulrich
William Waddell & Linda Rubel
William Waddell & Linda Rubel,
in honor of Simah, Ethan, and Jeehye
Michael Waters & Mihaela Moscaliuc